The Plan

God Has a Plan and It Includes YOU!

COLLEEN F. ASH

ILLUSTRATED BY VELMA K. BUTLER

LIFEWISE BOOKS

The Plan
God Has a Plan and It Includes YOU!

Published by:

⚙ LIFEWISE BOOKS

PO BOX 1072
Pinehurst, TX 77362
LifeWiseBooks.com

Cover Design and Interior Layout | Yvonne Parks | PearCreative.ca

To contact the author | colleenash.theplan@neo.rr.com

ISBN (Hardcover): 978-1-947279-76-6
ISBN (Paperback): 978-1-947279-77-3
ISBN (Ebook): 978-1-947279-78-0

Dedication

To my grandson, John Daniel:

May you walk out God's plan
in the power of the Holy Spirit.

4

God has a plan.

"His destiny-plan for the earth stands sure. His forever-plan remains in place and will never fail."
PSALM 33:11 TPT

God's plan is for his son, Jesus Christ, to rule everywhere and in every heart.

"And this is the plan: At the right time he will bring everything together under the authority of Christ - everything in heaven and on earth."

EPHESIANS 1:10 NLT

One of the most important parts of God's plan
was to send Jesus to earth.

*Jesus "…became human and
made his home among us."*

JOHN 1:14 NLT

While on earth, Jesus was both God and human.

"…in Christ lives all the fullness of God
in a human body."
COLOSSIANS 2:9 NLT

When Jesus became human, he set aside his outward glory of being God's son. He wanted to show us how a human being could live for God.

Jesus "…emptied himself of his outward glory by reducing himself to the form of a lowly servant. He became human!"

PHILIPPIANS 2:7 TPT

When Jesus grew up, he needed to be baptized.

"Then Jesus left Galilee to come to the Jordan to be baptized by John... Jesus replied, 'It is only right to do all that God requires.' Then John baptized Jesus. And as Jesus rose up out of the water, the heavenly realm opened up over him and he saw the Holy Spirit descend out of the heavens and rest upon him in the form of a dove."

MATTHEW 3:13,15-16 TPT

15

After Jesus was baptized, he announced the coming of God's Kingdom.

"…Jesus went into Galilee, where he preached God's Good News. 'The time promised by God has come at last!' he announced. 'The Kingdom of God is near!'"

MARK 1:14-15 NLT

17

Then Jesus began doing all kinds of miracles such as walking on water,

"...a strong wind began to blow and was stirring up the waters. The disciples had rowed about halfway across the lake when all of a sudden they caught sight of Jesus walking on top of the waves, coming toward them."

JOHN 6:18-19 TPT

…feeding 5000 hungry people from only a tiny amount of bread and fish,

"Then he had everyone sit down on the grass as he took the five loaves and two fish. He looked up into heaven, gave thanks to God, and broke the bread into pieces. He then gave it to his disciples, who in turn gave it to the crowds. And everyone ate until they were satisfied, for the food was multiplied in front of their eyes!"

MATTHEW 14:19-20 TPT

21

...healing everyone around him who was sick,

"A vast crowd brought to him people who were lame, blind, crippled, those who couldn't speak, and many others. They laid them before Jesus, and he healed them all."

MATTHEW 15:30 NLT

…and removing God's enemies from people's lives by the power of the Holy Spirit.

"One day Jesus cast out a demon from a man who couldn't speak, and when the demon was gone, the man began to speak. The crowds were amazed."

Jesus said, "…if I drive out demons by the power of the Spirit of God, then the end of Satan's kingdom has come!"

LUKE 11:14 NLT, MATTHEW 12:28 TPT

It is important to know that God was the one performing the miracles through Jesus.

"Jesus, the Victorious, was a man on a divine mission whose authority was clearly proven. For you know how God performed many powerful miracles, signs, and wonders through him."

ACTS 2:22 TPT

28

Then God's plan was for the apostles to begin
telling everyone about his Kingdom.

*"The apostles went out announcing
the good news everywhere."*
MARK 16:20 TPT

There was more for the apostles to do and they needed the Holy Spirit to do it.

"And now I will send the Holy Spirit, just as my Father promised. But stay here in the city until the Holy Spirit comes and fills you with power from heaven."

LUKE 24:49 NLT

After the apostles were filled with the Holy Spirit,
they did powerful miracles for God.

*"The apostles performed many signs, wonders, and
miracles among the people…when people knew
Peter was going to walk by, they carried the sick out
to the streets and laid them down on cots and mats,
knowing the incredible power emanating from him
would overshadow them and heal them…. and
everyone was healed!"*

ACTS 5:12,15-16 TPT

34

The apostles were humble because they knew the power to do God's work came from the Holy Spirit, not from themselves.

"The apostle Paul said: 'I've operated in God's miracle power with great humility' and 'we don't see ourselves as capable enough to do anything in our own strength, for our true competence flows from God's empowering presence.'"

ACTS 20:19, 2 CORINTHIANS 3:5 TPT

God's plan includes us.

"Before we were even born, he gave us our destiny; that we would fulfill the plan of God who always accomplishes every purpose and plan in his heart."

EPHESIANS 1:11 TPT

God's plan for us starts with us believing in Jesus.

*"The work you can do for God starts with
believing in the One he has sent."*
JOHN 6:29 TPT

In God's plan, He gives us important things to do. Like Jesus and the apostles, we are called to announce God's Kingdom, too.

"As you go into all the world, preach openly the wonderful news of the gospel to the entire human race!"

MARK 16:15 TPT

As believers, we are called to do miracles for God.

"And these miracle signs will accompany those who believe...they will lay hands on the sick and heal them."

MARK 16:17-18 TPT

God, please fill me now with the Holy Spirit so
I can share your message, your great love, and
your power with everyone I meet. In Jesus' name,
Amen!

*"…give us, your servants, great boldness in preaching your
word. Stretch out your hand with healing power; may
miraculous signs and wonders be done through the name
of your holy servant Jesus."*

ACTS 4:29-30 NLT

Declarations
(use each child's name)

_____ believes the Lord.

God fills _____ with the Holy Spirit.

God fills _____ with love for others.

God helps _____ tell Jesus' message of salvation, freedom, healing, and peace.

God gives _____ power to serve him well.

God does miracles through _____ by the power of the Holy Spirit in the name of Jesus.

About the Author

Colleen Ash is a wife, mother, grandmother, and an ordained minister of the gospel of Jesus Christ who has worked in corporate America for over 30 years. She is a member of Church Upon the Rock, Women in Ministry Network, and Joan Hunter Ministries - 4 Corners Alliance. Colleen resides in Hartville, Ohio with her husband John.

colleenash.theplan@neo.rr.com

About the Illustrator

Velma Butler is an illustrator and gifted artist. Her art is an expression of who she is and what God created her to be; expressive, innovative and imaginative. She is a member of the Next Chapter Church and Women in Ministry Network. Velma resides in Cincinnati with her husband, Tom, and is the proud mother of Jasmine and Drake.

velmie525@outlook.com

Works Cited

New Living Translation Bible. Tyndale House, 2015. *BibleGateway.com,*
www.biblegateway.com/versions/New-Living-Translation-NLT-Bible/

The Passion Translation Bible. BroadStreet, 2017. *BibleGateway.com,*
www.biblegateway.com/versions/The-Passion-Translation-TPT-Bible/#vinfo

CPSIA information can be obtained
at www.ICGtesting.com
Printed in the USA
LVHW072104220419
615088LV00018B/691/P